The Power Cut

Written by Samantha Montgomerie

Illustrated by Alfredo Belli

Collins

The rain patters. The night howls.

The power cuts off.

Dad looks for a torch.

We sit with Mum.

The room lights up.

6

We look for patterns with Mum.

Mum tells a yarn.

A goat sings to a cow.

Mum bows.

My cheeks hurt as Alex and I howl.

The power turns on.

We yell, "Turn off the lights!"

The power cut

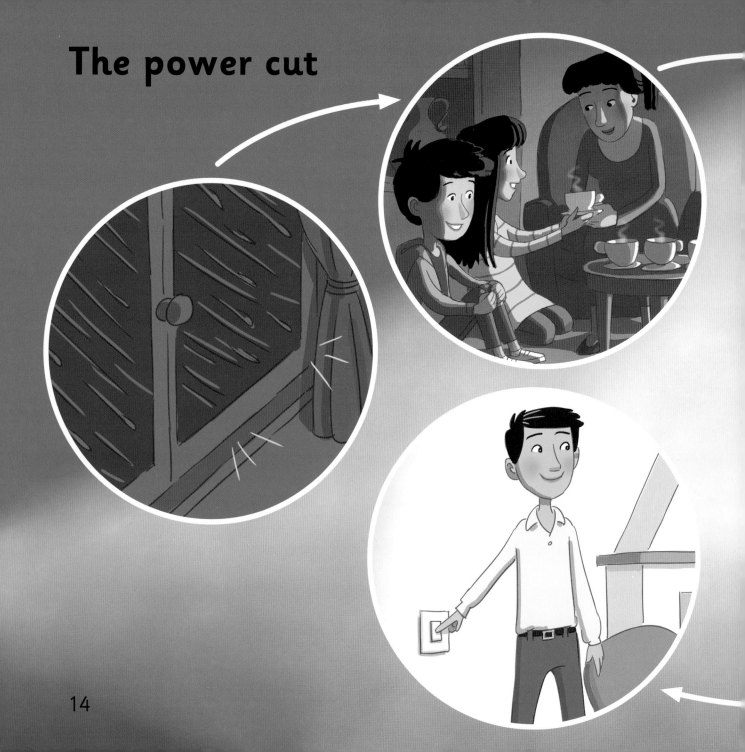

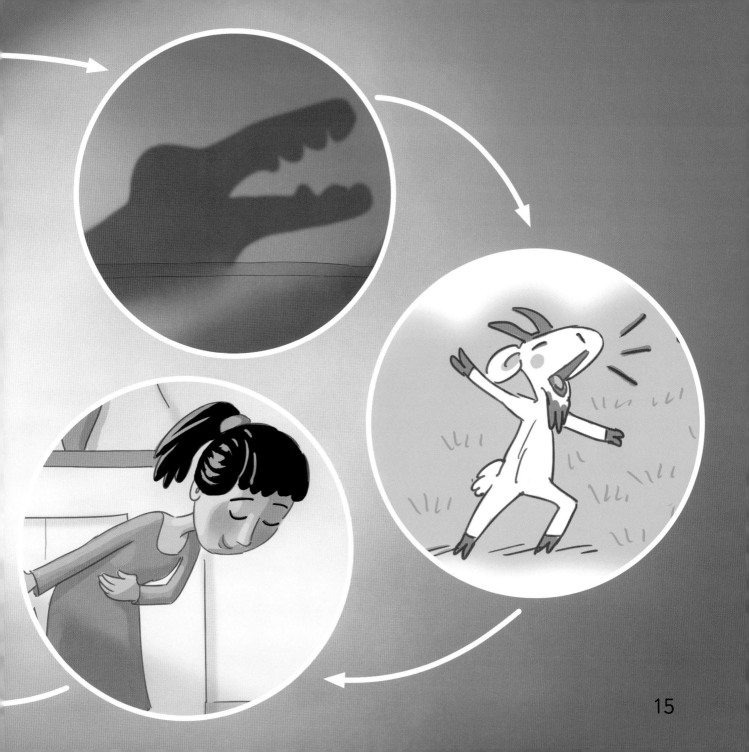

15

After reading

Letters and Sounds: Phase 3

Word count: 59

Focus phonemes: /ai/ /ee/ /igh/ /oa/ /oo/ /oo/ /ar/ /or/ /ur/ /ow/ /er/

Common exception words: the, and, I, to, we, my

Curriculum links: Understanding the World: The World

Early learning goals: Reading: use phonic knowledge to decode regular words and read them aloud accurately; demonstrate understanding when talking with others about what they have read

Developing fluency

- Your child may enjoy hearing you read the book. Model fluency and expression.
- Encourage your child to sound talk and then blend the words, e.g. t/ur/n **turn**. It may help to point to each sound as your child reads.
- Then ask your child to reread the sentence to support fluency and understanding.
- Practise reading page 13 with expression. Discuss how the children are saying the sentence. (*they are yelling*)

Phonic practice

- Ask your child to sound talk and blend each of the following words: n/igh/t, l/igh/t, ch/ee/k/s, p/a/tt/er/s, t/or/ch
- Can they find the words in the story that have a /igh/ sound in them? (*night, lights*)
- Can they think of any words that rhyme with **night**? (e.g. *light, sight, fright, bright, fight, might, tight, height*)

Extending vocabulary

- Ask your child:
  - On page 8, Mum tells a **yarn**. What other words could you use for yarn? (e.g. *story, tale*)
  - On page 7, the children look for **patterns**. What other words could you use for patterns? (e.g. *shapes, pictures, images, outlines*)